I0437332

# Your Life is Waiting:

## The Average Joe's Guide to Overcoming Panic Attacks and Anxiety

## Rafe R. Martin

authorHOUSE®

*AuthorHouse™*
*1663 Liberty Drive, Suite 200*
*Bloomington, IN 47403*
*www.authorhouse.com*
*Phone: 1-800-839-8640*

*© 2007 Rafe R. Martin. All rights reserved.*

*No part of this book may be reproduced, stored in
a retrieval system, or transmitted by any means
without the written permission of the author.*

*First published by AuthorHouse 10/1/2007*

*ISBN: 978-1-4343-1680-6 (sc)*

*Printed in the United States of America
Bloomington, Indiana*

*This book is printed on acid-free paper.*

# Contents

## Dedication

To Sherry, my compass.

## Acknowledgements

Thanks to Scott Greeson for asking me for three years when this book would be done. The first copy is yours.

# Preface

We all take the simple joys of life for granted, until the day when they are snatched away from us. During the first months of my battle with panic and anxiety, I can remember the feelings of envy towards everyone around me that could function normally and enjoy life. I wanted what they had and would have given everything I owned to be able to live a normal life again.

I emerged from a three-year struggle with anxiety disorder as a new person ready to take on anything the world could throw at me. I'm now compelled to help as many people as I can who are facing the same struggle with panic and anxiety. I know from experience that having someone that has been through it and overcame it is the best beacon of hope that you can have when you are in the trenches battling this thing.

My heart and soul have been burdened with writing this book for some time, because I know that sharing my experience will help someone out there get well. This is my gift of hope to all those that are suffering through the crippling grip of panic and anxiety. In the first part of this book, I share my experiences and methods of overcoming this condition. The last part of the book will help you come up with your own plan to get well. Read this book in good faith and know that you are not alone.

# Introduction

This book is written for people who are suffering from anxiety disorder, panic attacks, or agoraphobia. It is a personal account of my experiences and how I overcame panic disorder and agoraphobia without medication and regained a normal lifestyle. If you're looking for a medical analysis of your condition or want to delve into the ocean of theories on why you may be genetically prone to having an anxiety disorder, then this is not the book for you. Genetic predisposition or not, if you're serious about returning to a life that is not ruled by fear, this book will serve as a guide to help you put a plan together to get your life back to normal.

As you read, you will notice that I use the phrase "get your life back" frequently. What I mean by that is returning to a life that is not ruled by fear. After reading this book, you might discover that you do not want your old life, meaning your old self, back. If you're like me, you'll realize that this life-changing experience has made you a better person than you were before you succumbed to panic. You'll probably like yourself a lot better after you come out the other end of this transformation because you will understand what was wrong with your old life that led you to the place where you are now.

**Disclaimer:** It is strongly recommended that you have a thorough examination by a medical doctor to determine whether or not your symptoms (i.e. chest pains, dizziness, shortness of breath, fainting, etc.) are a result of a medical condition. Please follow the advice of your physician.

If you're like me, you've probably been told that you're in perfect physical condition and that you are suffering from anxiety, panic disorder, or agoraphobia. You may have been told, like I was, that your body is completely healthy but you have a "chemical imbalance" in your brain that is the cause of your panic or agoraphobia. You may have even been told that it runs in your family and that you're just going to have to get used to it. As the son of a man that took Xanax for twenty-five years, I'm here as living proof that anyone with the will to get well can get well.

I'm not a doctor or psychiatrist. I have no medical training or certifications in counseling. I don't claim to be an expert on anxiety or panic disorder, but I do have a good understanding of what it is, what causes it, and how to treat it. I am just a regular guy who has lived through the disabling grip of panic attacks and fear and overcame it to return to a normal life.

# My Story

Let me start by telling you a little bit about myself so that you might better understand where I came from and how we probably aren't all that different from each other. Hopefully, as you find out who I am, you will see that you don't have to be someone special to overcome this crippling condition.

I'm a typical middle-class citizen. I came from a fairly normal home. My brother and I both had what I consider "normal" childhoods; our parents both worked, and we always had nice clothes and plenty of toys and things to keep us happy. We lived in a modest home in a good neighborhood and went to church regularly. We weren't the Cleavers, but I'd say we had it better than most kids.

Although my parents preached it to me, I had no interest in making good grades or applying myself in school. I never found school to be hard, but I did find it boring. I managed to squeak through high school with average grades. After high school I went to three colleges and changed majors two times before I finally gave up. I didn't know what I wanted to do with my life, and my parents had gotten tired of paying the bill for me to do nothing but party.

I got married at age twenty-two to my wife, Sherry. I'm not sure what she saw in me at the time; I felt like I was coasting along from one day to the next. We were both uncertain about our careers. After trying my hand as a real estate salesman, car salesman, and even door-to-door salesman of frozen foods for the first three years of my marriage, I realized that I had better get serious about something for a change. It was time to apply myself if I wanted to have a future, so I decided to go back to school to study computer programming.

I worked my way through college as a computer technician and got a degree in business computer programming. I was the president of the data processing club and graduated with high honors, quite a change from my earlier college days. I had finally applied myself for once and realized my true potential.

Fast forward twelve years: I have been working in the computer and internet industry for the last twelve years as a web designer and programmer, and several years ago I partnered with a long-time friend and started an internet consulting firm. My wife and I have two beautiful children that keep us busy and grandparents that keep them spoiled. I'd say I have it pretty good, especially when you consider that at one point in my life fear kept me from doing something as simple as going to the grocery store.

If I were you reading this book right now, I wouldn't be able to put a lot of stock in some guy's advice on how to overcome panic and anxiety unless I felt that I could relate to his experience. *What experience? Maybe he just had a panic attack or two.* Maybe you're thinking to yourself, *I'm different. No one could possibly understand what I'm going through.* That's why I feel it is important that I tell you my story, starting with my first panic attack.

## My First Panic Attack

Forging your career path in the technology industry can be very demanding. If you want to be successful, you have to stay on the cutting edge. That means continually educating yourself and trying to stay one step ahead of everyone else. At the time my panic trouble started, I had high ambitions and put pressure on myself to meet my career goals. I thought I could do it all, at times taking on more than I could handle.

I had just landed my first real job in my new career working for IBM as a software engineer, and there was so much opportunity with this new job. It was an exciting time in my life. We had just moved from our small town to a bigger city so I could be closer to work. In a few months I had already advanced into a higher position. Along with the pay raise came more responsibility, but I loved it and wanted even more.

For the first time in my life, I was making a respectable salary. Looking back, it wasn't really a lot of money, but I was doing well enough to support both of us while my wife went back to college. I was building computer systems on the side for extra money and had new clients calling me for work on a regular basis.

I was healthy. I worked out every day. I had a good marriage. We were in a new city that offered culture and new experiences. Between all that and my new job, it was a bit overwhelming, but exciting nonetheless. My life couldn't have been more perfect.

Then came the day I'll never forget, the day of my first panic attack. It was a lazy summer Saturday. I didn't have to be anywhere or do anything important all day. My wife Sherry and I were both excited about going to a concert later that night. We hung around our apartment most of the morning, had breakfast, and decided to go to the local mall, shop, and grab some lunch at the food court. We took our time getting showered and dressed and finally headed out to the mall.

We were excited about the concert later that evening and were talking about our plans for the night as I drove us to the mall, which was only about ten minutes from our apartment. I distinctly remember approaching a red light as we got close to the entrance. Slowing down to stop for the light, I had this sudden overwhelming feeling that something was wrong. My heart began to pound like it was going to explode! I got short of breath and was turning pale. Sherry realized that something was going on and asked if I was ok. I told her I didn't know what was going on and that my chest was pounding and I was getting dizzy. I sat there for a moment wondering what to do. We were about a hundred yards from the mall entrance, so I decided to pull into the mall parking lot for a minute to collect myself.

By the time I got the car parked, the symptoms had gone away. I just shrugged it off as we walked into the mall and headed toward the food court. We talked about it as we were standing in line to place our order. I thought that maybe I was just hungry and needed something to eat. Sherry thought that maybe it was a panic attack. Whatever it was, I knew that it scared me for that brief moment that it lasted, and I didn't want it to happen again.

We waited in line, got our food, and were walking towards a table. As I sat down, my heart began to pound again. *Oh no, it's back!* I thought. I made it to my seat and told Sherry what was happening. I sat there for a moment trying to get a grip on myself and figure out what was going on. Whatever it was, it was not going away but rather getting worse by the minute. I sat there with my heart racing, breathing fast. My lips began to go numb, my arms and feet were tingling, and I had this feeling that something terrible was about to happen. Something was definitely wrong. It was surreal, almost as if I were not in my own body, but watching this take place from a distance. *I'm having a heart attack*, I thought. *I need to get out of here and get to the hospital!* I tried to stand up but couldn't feel my legs. I couldn't feel my arms or anything. I couldn't even open my mouth to speak because I couldn't feel my lips. I was stuck there! *What is happening to me? Is this it?*

*Am I about to die right here in this food court? Dear God, help me!*

I was paralyzed with fear, scared to move from that seat. Sherry was getting very concerned now, and her fear just added to mine. *What am I going to do? Should we call for help? Someone is going to have to physically carry me to the car. I can't walk. Wait, this is crazy.* I was trying to focus and pull myself together, but by this time I was a mental wreck. The heart racing was now coming and going in waves. I was regaining the feeling in my arms and legs and could finally talk. Sherry urged me to get up, but I didn't want to move from that seat. If I moved, I would die right there in front of everyone. I decided to sit there until I felt like I could get up and walk. We sat there for probably another ten minutes, but it seemed like hours.

I finally got the courage together to get up from the booth. As we walked out of the mall, I started feeling bad again. I felt that if I could just make it to the car, I would be alright. *The car, the car, just make it to the car.* When we got in the car, Sherry asked if I wanted to go to the emergency room. I told her, "No, but take me to get a six pack!" I thought that maybe a few beers would calm my nerves and make whatever this was go away.

We got my beer and headed back to the apartment, and I was still rattled about what had happened. I drank a few beers and tried to relax, but I could not stop thinking about it. We decided that I had probably just experienced an anxiety attack, but I still wasn't sure. I had heard people talk about anxiety attacks and that sometimes they are mistaken for heart attacks. If it was just a case of nerves, then I had nothing to worry about: I could deal with stress.

So off we went to the concert. The traffic going into the place was backed up for miles. While we were waiting to get in, the car overheated. *Great. This is my day.* Luckily, there was a man watering his yard close by, and I got the radiator filled up using his water hose. That problem was solved. Nothing was going to stop me from getting to this concert that I had been looking forward to for months.

We finally made it to the concert, got a couple of drinks, and found our seats. I was going to have a good time despite the day I was having thus far. The anticipation was building. The main act was about to come on, and the seats around us were starting to fill up. The next thing I know, two guys sat down beside me and start loading up their pipe, and they weren't using tobacco. Not being a drug user, I was offended by the marijuana use just inches from me, but I decided to enjoy myself nonetheless. Everyone stood and cheered as the main act came out on stage. The music started. The crowd roared. The marijuana smoke blew in my face. Then the symptoms came back.

Here it was again, a repeat of the mall incident that had just happened a few hours earlier. I was going numb all over, my heart was racing, and my breathing got fast and short. I was scared. *This can't be!* All this time waiting for this concert and now this happens. I thought, *I won't allow it.* I didn't want to spoil it for Sherry. It had gone away earlier, so maybe it will go away this time. But it didn't. I held out for a few minutes, and then I started getting really scared. I couldn't take it anymore. I thought it was a heart attack, so we left for the hospital.

This was really it. I thought this was really the end of my life. Here we were, speeding towards the hospital, hoping I can make it. *The hospital, just make it to the hospital, and the doctors will save you.* My heart felt like it was in my throat. I had sharp, shooting chest pains and was dizzy. I was clenching my seatbelt, the dashboard, anything I could get a grip on. *What is happening to me?*

We made it to the emergency room, and the staff took me right into an exam room. The doctor rushed in and started asking me questions as he and a nurse wired me up to an EKG machine. Relieved to be there, I started feeling better right away just because I knew that I was in the hospital and would be safe there.

After checking me over and concluding that nothing was physically wrong with me, he asked me some questions about my job, family, and marriage. He told me that I had just had an anxiety attack and that it sounded like I had been under a lot of stress lately. I felt better already. "That's just nerves," I said. "I can deal with that." So the doctor gave me a clean bill of health and sent me home. He suggested that I go see my regular physician as soon as possible to get a thorough examination and to let him know what had happened.

I went home from the emergency room feeling relieved that the terrible day was over and hopeful that I had seen the end of panic attacks. I was definitely going to try to reduce my stress so I wouldn't have to suffer through the misery of another one. I had a hard time sleeping that night and ended up spending most of the night on the couch with the television on, trying to keep my mind off that day's events. The next day was Sunday, so I knew that I'd have a full day to recover before returning to work on Monday.

## Fear Setting In

After a miserable night on the couch tossing and turning and getting only a couple hours of sleep, I woke up the next morning to find myself trembling all over. Very uneasy with a strange tightness in my chest, I sat down at the dining room table to have breakfast and just stared at my food. I couldn't eat. I had absolutely no appetite. All I could think about was when the next panic attack was going to hit me. To me, another attack was inevitable.

I was tired and confused and needed to rest, so I got in bed and tried to get some sleep. Every time I would get to the point of falling asleep, I would suddenly wake up. It was the strangest feeling: it was as if my body would not let me sleep for fear of dying, almost like some built-in mechanism for keeping me alive. I tried again and again to overcome it and just fall asleep, but something would not let me. I began to think that if I fell asleep, I would stop breathing and never wake up. What a helpless mess I was, exhausted, and now suddenly scared to sleep.

*What is this all about? Yesterday morning at this time, I was perfectly ok. How can this be? Yesterday I was normal and today I'm scared to go to sleep. This is crazy. I'm just going to ignore whatever this is and go to sleep.* So I lay there for another couple of hours trying to talk myself into feeling better, but it didn't work.

As much as I hate hospitals and doctors, I called the doctor that had seen me the night before in the emergency room. I told him that I couldn't eat or sleep. Then something happened that I think set the course of events to come. He asked me if I was afraid to go anywhere. "What do you mean, afraid?" Then he went on to explain to me that some people who have panic attacks get to the point of being afraid to go anywhere for fear of having another attack. "No, I'm not afraid to go anywhere." I told him. "That's the silliest thing I've ever heard. I just can't eat or sleep, and I really need to get some rest so I can work tomorrow."

He called in a Xanax prescription for me. I had heard of it but never took any. I hated taking pills for anything, and I still do, but I was at a point of desperation. I had to eat, and I had to sleep. I felt terrible. So, being the anti-pill popper that I am, I cut the pill in half and only took one half of it. Within ten minutes I felt so good that I questioned whether or not I ever felt bad in the first place. Within 20 minutes I was ready to eat everything I could get my hands on. I ate a huge meal and went to sleep. I didn't have a bit of trouble getting to sleep. No more fear.

I slept right through the night until the alarm clock woke me the next morning.

It was Monday morning and time for me to forget the terrible weekend I had just been through and get back to my normal routine. I pulled myself out of bed, still tired but ready to get up and get on with the day. As I got ready for work, I started feeling a little anxious, hoping that I had seen the last of panic and all the experiences that came with it.

The apartment we were renting was conveniently located right next to Interstate 40, which is the major freeway in the area and was the most direct route to my job. One turn out of the driveway and I found myself amidst the thousands of rat racers on their way to work in the Monday morning stop-and-go rush hour madness. The stretch of road I had to take to work was notorious for being bottlenecked with bumper-to-bumper road-raged drivers.

As I sat there in the gridlock, I began to realize that I was alone in my car and that if I had another one of those panic attacks, no one was around to help me. I was over those panic attacks, right? *But wait, what if they do come back? Am I sure that I'm over them? What will I do? I know,*

*I'll just pull over and call home if I start to feel it coming on.* So I got in the right lane because I could pull over to the shoulder quickly if I needed to. I proceeded to work, riding in the right lane all the way there.

I made it to work. I felt better knowing that the drive was over. IBM had a huge facility, and I had a long walk from the parking lot to my cubicle. I would use that time walking to my desk to plan my day, thinking of things that needed to be done that day. My plan for this day was to go to my cubicle and try to keep a low profile all day and forget this panic thing.

Feeling good about my plan, taking a few deep breaths, I opened the door to the lab where I worked. I looked over to my desk to find my manager and three of my coworkers waiting for me. "Oh, I'm glad you're here. I've got two new projects to kick off and you're the project lead for both. Here's your team." In that instant I felt my heart race and my head get light and tingly. Everyone was looking at me, waiting for a response. I was spiraling into a panic attack, right there in front of all of them. I stumbled to my seat and sat down, holding my chest. I was trying to hide what was going on, but it was evident that something was wrong with me. Julie, my manager, asked if I was feeling alright. "I've got to go. I can't handle this today. I'll call you. I'm going home." Everyone looked at me in shock and disbelief as I got up and started out the door. My head was spinning with fear and anger because this was happening to me again. I was struggling to keep this panic attack from spiraling out of control like the first one did. I tried to think about something else, but I couldn't. I felt doomed. I was getting scared. But why? I wasn't in any danger. I felt like I would be fine once I got to the car.

I made it back to my car, got in and sat there. I was scared, confused, and mad that this was happening. *What is wrong with me? Am I having a heart attack or what? Why me?* The same sensations I had just had two nights before were back again. But this time there was a new feeling in the mix, a feeling of vulnerability and helplessness. I wanted to be home. I felt like I would be fine if I could just get home.

I sat there and tried to compose myself. I thought about what the doctor had told me – that I was perfectly healthy. My heart checked out fine. This was not a heart attack, but a panic attack. But there must be something wrong with me. Why did I feel scared? Then it hit me: I was scared of the panic attack itself, not of having a heart attack. I was scared of having the experience that I had at the mall, that feeling of impending doom and helplessness.

I started the trip home. Remembering my concern about being able to pull over quickly, I drove in the right lane all the way home. I found that as I got farther away from work, my anxiety started to get worse. I turned on the radio and tried to sing along to get my mind off the way I was feeling. Once I had sight of my apartment building, my anxiety started to lighten up. I couldn't get there fast enough. I raced into the parking lot and parked my car quickly. I was home and felt better already.

My wife was very surprised to see me home. I told her about the meeting in my cube at work and how I started to feel another attack coming on, but I didn't tell her about driving in the right lane; I felt embarrassed about that because it seemed like such a silly thing to do.

The day had just become a repeat of the previous Saturday. I sat on the couch watching TV and trying to rest and get my mind off the way I felt. I tried to eat now and then but had no appetite, just like before. I spent that night trying to sleep but couldn't, just like before.

The pattern repeated but worsened every day, and I called in sick for the next two weeks. Night after night, I lay awake tossing and turning, scared that I would stop breathing. My fear of having another panic attack had suddenly taken control of my life. I would venture out of the house occasionally and find myself rushing home due to overwhelming fear. I had gone from driving in the right lane all the time to not driving at all, having my wife drive me everywhere.

Every few days, I would feel like I could handle going back to work, so Sherry would drop me off. I would stay a few hours until it got unbearable and call her to pick me up. I stayed home three or four days out of the week. This went on for six weeks.

I was scared of losing my job, so I figured I had better try to explain myself to my boss. I told her what I was going through and that I needed a little time to get back on track. She was very understanding and assured me that my job wasn't going anywhere, but she was concerned about me falling behind on my work.

I had started down a one-way road to helplessness. Not only was I sick, but I was also depressed and worried about missing work. I was an hourly-waged employee; I got a very good hourly rate when I was working, but I had no paid vacation or sick days. So that meant if I wasn't working, I wasn't getting paid. After all this missed work, I was running out of money in a hurry. With little to no income, and what little savings I had managed to hold on to now depleted, we were faced with no other choice than to move in with my in-laws. I thank God for them; I don't know what we would have done without parents to fall back on. I sucked up my pride, and we took a weekend to move back to our hometown.

The day of the move turned out to be another memorable day in my life. That was the day of my worst panic attack. I had rented a moving truck , and my brother and my in-laws were all there helping us get everything packed and onto the truck. Feeling unusually bold for some reason, I decided to drive the truck with my brother riding along.

We started the 45-minute trip down the interstate. Everything was going well until we got out in the country, five miles from the nearest exit. I felt the panic coming on in a hurry but managed to get the truck pulled over on the shoulder. I had all the symptoms as before, but they seemed stronger than ever. My brother was seeing all of this for the first time and didn't know quite how to take it. He just watched me in helpless amazement as I went through the routine: the tingling in my hands and feet, the lips going numb, the hyperventilation, the dizziness, the panic.

This attack was so severe that I really thought I would not live through it. Here I was, pulled over on the side of the road in the middle of nowhere with no phone, no doctors, nowhere near a hospital or any form of help. *But wait, my pills!* I pulled the bottle from my pocket and stared at it for a few moments contemplating the consequences of taking one of them. I felt like it was my only option at the time. My brother was sitting there with me urging me to take one. He felt as helpless as I did. So in my moment of profound desperation, I took the pill. Thirty minutes later, with my brother at the wheel, we made it to our destination.

That day my self-esteem had reached a new low. I felt like I had failed everyone's expectation of me. Here we were, moving in with my in-laws because I had no income. However, it was quite a relief for me to know that we could stay there as long as we needed. Not having all the bills associated with an overpriced apartment would take some of the stress off. On the flip side, when I finally got up the nerve to go back to work, I had a 45-minute commute to deal with. That's a long time to be in the car by yourself when you're terrified of driving.

## Fear Controlling My Life

We got settled in at my in-laws', and I spent the next few months in and out of work because of more and more difficulty with fear and panic symptoms. The 45-minute commute was like waking up every day and having to fight a fire-breathing dragon: it stared me in the face every morning and mocked me. There were good days and bad days, but the bad days seemed to increasingly outnumber the good ones. Fear ruled my life and every move I made. I started off every day dreading everything from the drive to work, to lunch, to meetings, and any other situation in which I wasn't totally in control. My life was a continual struggle to overcome the day's challenges without having a full-blown panic attack.

I had developed "safe zones." These were places where I felt comfortable, and less susceptible to panic. My best safe zone was at home or anywhere near it, and my next best safe zone was my cubicle at work. I could get into my own little corner there and have some level of privacy and be inconspicuous.

I always seemed to feel safe in my car as long as it was parked, either at work or at home. The farther away from my safe zones I got, the worse I would feel. I could feel the grip of fear tighten in proportion to the distance I was away from a safe zone. I found it harder and harder to do simple things like going to the grocery store. First of all, most of the stores were out of my safe zones. Secondly, I got panicked any time I had to stand in a line, even if there was only one person in front of me. I couldn't stand the thought of being confined to an area for any length of time; I had to be able to get out quickly. There were many times that I'd just leave the store if I couldn't check out right away because I would get so panicked waiting in line.

I didn't want to have an attack in a public place, especially in front of total strangers. Sometimes I would find myself forced to stand in the checkout line, so I would do things to occupy my mind like counting floor tiles or reading the ingredients on all the candy wrappers on the rack. I liked to make up complex math problems and try to solve them while I was waiting in line, anything to absorb my thoughts and keep me from going into panic.

Driving had become a nightmare for me. I had to always drive in the right lane. I would speed because I wanted to get back to my nearest safe zone as quickly as possible, and

I dreaded red lights to the point that I would get panicky every time I had to stop for one. I would turn on the radio and try to sing along, or count cars going by, anything to keep my mind from dwelling on panic.

I developed a fear of going to the cafeteria at work. I would only go after the lunchtime rush was over when I thought I had the best chances of getting in and out quickly. And I always got my meals to go, bringing them back to my desk to eat. The few times that I had gone down there to eat with coworkers were disasters. I would feel so much anxiety in the crowded dining area that I would have to make up a quick excuse and get out right away.

I mapped out the shortest routes to the hospitals from both work and home just so I would be prepared in case of an attack. If I found myself out of my usual safe zones, I would try to work out the fastest routes back to my house or to the nearest hospital and get a tentative plan together just in case panic set in.

I had to stop working out because exercise causes increased heart rate, and I had associated that sensation with panic. Something as simple as walking up stairs could send me into the pre-stages of a panic attack because my heart would race, and that could send me spiraling into a full-blown panic attack. So I started avoiding stairs, or if it became absolutely necessary to climb stairs, I did it very slowly so as to not get my heart rate up.

I started to carry my prescription bottle of Xanax in my pocket at all times, and it became my crutch. I knew that if it came right down to it, I could pop a Xanax and feel better in a matter of minutes. The big problem with that solution was that when the Xanax wore off, I would feel worse than I did before I took it. For that reason, I rarely took any. I think I took a grand total of three pills in the months I was incapacitated because I felt so much worse after the pill wore off, and I didn't want to become addicted if I could help it. I carried the bottle with me all the time, and it became an item in my panic first aid kit, which I'll discuss later.

These are just a few examples of the countless ways my life was changing in order for me to make it through each day. Things that most people do without question were now obstacles to me. I had become a prisoner to fear.

## Physical Symptoms

When you get right down to the root of a panic attack, it's the physical sensations that cause the spiraling of events that lead into a full-blown panic attack. Some will say that the process is started by a mental trigger, a bad thought or idea that manifests itself physically, which then starts the cycle. You might get a flutter in your chest that causes you to be scared or concerned. That fear triggers other physical sensations, and so on. Before you know it, you've spiraled into a panic attack. Because I was so obsessed with the fear of having another panic attack, I was very in tune with my body and any subtle physical sensations or changes that I experienced. Imagine having a watchdog that is monitoring your vital statistics twenty-four hours a day. I was the watchdog over my own body, acutely aware of the slightest change in heart rate, breathing rate, temperature, and so on. Because of that, I lived in a state of generalized anxiety, elevated and lowered by my current conditions, and sometimes elevated to the point of panic.

The physical sensations that accompanied my anxiety and the onset of panic took on many forms. At first there were just a handful of symptoms such as tightness in my chest, tingling in my lips and extremities, and hyperventilation. It seemed that as I got used to these symptoms, which I had associated with panic attacks, a host of new symptoms would invade my body. These new symptoms would occur any time, not necessarily when I was feeling panicked. Some of the symptoms I experienced on a regular basis were dizziness, abdominal cramping, sharp chest pains, intense shooting pains in my head, twitching in my eyes, trembling, and burping. Yes, burping.

One of the scariest sensations I experienced frequently was tremors; the shaking was so bad, I actually felt like I was vibrating. This usually occurred in bed, and I remember asking Sherry if she felt the bed shaking because of the severity of the sensation. It seemed like I had a new physical sensation to deal with every few weeks, and each new one was scarier than the last.

## Emotional Effects

So where were my friends and family during all this? The fact is that I kept all of this to myself. They knew that I was sick, but they didn't really understand what was wrong with me or what I was experiencing. The only way I could describe it to my family was that I was having "nerve trouble." That was a term that they could relate to because in the 1970's my father had been through what they called a "nervous breakdown." You don't hear that term these days. Today it's called an anxiety attack or panic attack. Trying to explain what was happening to me seemed impossible, so I left it at that.

Because I was afraid of being labeled as mentally unstable, I didn't want to disclose the details of my living hell with anyone. As a man, I was embarrassed about my condition because it made me feel weak and inadequate. What would people think if they knew I drove in the right lane all the time or counted candy bars in the checkout line? Would people start to avoid me if they knew the silly things I did just to ward off a panic attack? I didn't want to take the risk, so I made up excuses to avoid social situations or any event that required me to leave my safe zones.

I remember giving in once and going to a movie with my friend Mike. I was nervous from the moment I hung up the phone with him, but my wife and I thought it would be good for me to get out. It was a disaster from the start. He drove, but I was on the verge of a panic attack the whole way to the theater. Once we got in, Mike insisted on sitting on the front row. I didn't even last through the coming attractions. I had to make up an excuse and flee to the back of the theater. After getting myself a drink and hiding on the back row for a few minutes, I went down to the front and told Mike that I was sick and needed to stay near the back close to the bathroom. I spent the entire time pacing around the lobby, waiting for the movie to end. I faked a stomach ache all the way home in order to hide the panic that was consuming me. Why didn't I just tell Mike from the beginning what was wrong with me? Maybe he would have understood and offered to sit somewhere else or even drive me home. I didn't want to be the party pooper, and I was too embarrassed to tell him what I was going through.

I felt cheated by the whole situation. *Why me? Why did I have to suffer with this condition?* It seemed so unfair to have to endure this misery day after day with no end in sight. I thought everyone else was normal. If they only knew how much they were taking for granted. I'd always heard people say that things happen for a reason and that everything always works out for the best. How could anything good come out of this? That seemed like a bunch of nonsense to me at the time, but today it all makes perfect sense. One day it will all make perfect sense to you, too.

My feelings of anger soon turned into depression. I wanted more than anything else in the world to be normal and to be my old self and do the things that I used to do without giving anything a second thought. I should have been able to drive to the store and stand in a checkout line. I should have been able to take my wife out to dinner without leaving in the middle of the meal because of panic. I couldn't do anything outside of my home without fear of having a panic attack. I had accepted that as a fact of life, and that belief created in me a deep depression.

## Hopelessness

I felt doomed to live with fear and to be confined to these safe zones that were getting smaller all the time. My activities had become so limited that my quality of life had diminished to a miserable existence. There were no signs of it getting better, only worse by the day. Desperately, I looked for someone who had overcome this condition and returned to a normal life, but there was no one. I needed some inspiration from someone who had been through what I was going through, and I would have given everything I owned just to hear from a recovered agoraphobic that I could get my life back. There was no one who understood my hell. I had reached the point of hopelessness.

So, here I was living with my in-laws. I was broke and unable to work. I felt like a burden to everyone around me. My safe zones had diminished to the point that I didn't want to go beyond the end of the street. I couldn't even drive my car around the block without going into panic. Before I knew it, I was down to only one safe zone—the house and yard.

My days consisted of sleeping late, trying to take a shower and get dressed without panicking, and sitting in front of the television or computer all day. I tried to watch something interesting or play computer games most of the time so that I wouldn't dwell on the horde of physical symptoms I experienced continually. If I thought too much about how terrible I felt, I would get worked up into a state of heightened anxiety, which made me more susceptible to having a full blown panic attack.

My nights consisted of lying in bed shaking, clutching my pillow, and asking God, "Why me?" until finally falling asleep. I eventually got to the point that I didn't even care about getting out of the bed at all. I slept all the time because the only time I didn't feel bad was when I was sleeping. I started to think that I could sleep this whole thing away and that one day I would wake up and be my old self again. But every day that I woke up, my first thought was about the fear and the dread, so I'd go back to sleep some more and hope that it would all go away.

I had slipped into a deep, dark, depressing existence. All the things I used to do and places I used to go were now impossible for me to enjoy. I envied all the normal people of the world, and I felt doomed to live like a hermit for the rest of my life. *Was this punishment for something I had done? How can this be happening to me? Maybe this is just a bad dream and I'll wake up tomorrow as a normal person.* But every day I woke up farther in misery and despair.

My safe zones were now smaller than ever. One of the few things I could manage to do every day was walk to the mailbox at the end of the driveway. Now, even that was too far out of my safe zone. I had spun a cocoon for myself that consisted of the bedroom and the bathroom and sometimes the kitchen. This ever-shrinking safe zone was quickly getting out of control. I was certain that I would be bed-ridden in a matter of weeks. I started to worry about the future. I couldn't live with my in-laws forever. *Could my wife support us? What kind of man was I for letting this happen?*

## Making the Decision to Change

I pulled myself out of bed around noon one day and was on my way to the mailbox. This was one of the few remaining activities that I could perform that allowed me to maintain a manageable level of anxiety. This particular morning, I found myself standing on the edge of the front porch staring at the mailbox, scared to take another step. The twenty-yard walk to the mailbox was something that

I had been able to do every day. But, over the past few weeks, I had slowly started to become more and more anxious about it. Now the anxiety over walking out there by myself had grown to the point that I couldn't do it without consideration. I was too scared to step off the front porch. As I stood there contemplating taking that first step, my body was overcome with physical panic symptoms. I felt a full-blown panic attack coming on, and my first reaction was to immediately turn around and get back into my bed.

Rather than going into the house and getting into bed, I sat down on the top step of the porch in an effort to calm down. Staring at the mailbox, I started to reflect on my situation. For the first time since all of this "nerve trouble" started, I took a look at myself from the outside. My emotions were all over the place. I sat there for a long while in self-pity, thinking about how unfair this was. I had lost my life. I didn't deserve this. As I thought about my former "normal" life, I got an aching pain in the gut, the kind of pain you feel when you think about losing a close relative or loved one. I thought of my former life, of all the fun things I had done before this started. I was happy, funny, and enjoyed being around friends and family. I missed being able to play golf, go to the movies, going out to eat, having date night with my wife, and all the romantic little silly things I used to do for her. I also missed working, having money, and being on top of my career. I had always planned to do something big, to be a self-made success at something that mattered and to have an impact on people. All of those ambitions seemed far-fetched now and impossible to a guy that was confined to three rooms at his in-laws' house.

I started to imagine what people that knew me would think of me if they could see me right now. If I were "normal" and had a friend who was behaving and living the way I was, I would think he'd lost it. What kind of person is scared to walk to the mailbox? What kind of person is too scared to drive a car or go to a shopping mall? What kind of man loses his job, goes broke, and moves in with his in-laws and never comes out of the house?

My self-pity turned to anger. Was I going to let this thing rob me of the life I wanted to live? It was not only robbing me of a normal life, but it was robbing my wife of a normal husband and a fulfilling marriage. It was ruining me on all fronts: personally, emotionally, and financially. What can I do to fix this? I can take pills, but I'll just get hooked on them. I don't want that, but it's better than what I've got now. At least I'll be able to function. But will I be my old self? I kept going back to the question:

how can I be normal one day and weeks later be sitting here like this? I'm sick of this! *You know what — I'm the one allowing this to happen, and I'm the only one that can do anything about it. Why can't I walk to the stupid mailbox? What am I scared of, death? I'm going to get up right now and march my crazy ass to the mailbox, and if it kills me, so what, I'M NOT LIVING ANYWAY!*

With the most determination I have ever had to do anything in my life, I got up and walked to that mailbox. The panic waves came like demons, but I didn't let them stop me. I kept going until I had reached my goal. I put my hand on the mailbox, looked up to God and said, "This is the day I get my life back!"

## Looking for Answers

I had made the decision to change but wasn't sure where to start or what to do next. I had so many questions. How can I be fine one day and screwed up the next? Had anyone ever been in my situation and returned to a normal life? If so, where do I find these people? How did they do it? What should my plan be? Are there others going through this right now? My search for answers led me to find a local anxiety and panic support group that met weekly. I was thrilled to find out about these people.

I thought *Oh boy, I'll go and meet someone that has been through this and can tell me how to get well.* I could hardly wait for the first meeting. *But wait, I have to leave my safe zone in order to attend the meeting. How am I going to make it to the meeting? I'm going to be out of my safe zone for a little while, but it's not really that far from the house. I'm just going to have to tough it out for an hour or so. I can do it. I have to do it.*

The day of the support group meeting finally came. Still scared to drive by myself, I had my wife drop me off at the meeting location. I was very nervous about being in a room full of strangers but excited about the prospect of meeting someone that could help me. As I walked into the room, everyone stopped what they were doing and focused on me. *Oh great, new blood,* I thought. The person that ran the meeting came over to me, and in a very soft and pleasant voice asked where I would like to sit that would make me the least nervous. Everyone's attention still on me, I replied, "How about the seat closest to the exit." That got a chuckle or two from the group. They were all very careful to make sure I was completely at ease, but all the attention was beginning to make me uncomfortable. I felt like I was on display and got a little panicky, but I managed to hide it well. Nothing was going to get me out of that room until I had some answers.

The meeting got under way, and everyone that was comfortable with speaking got to tell his or her story. I kept waiting for someone to tell a story of how he had overcome panic, or at least how she was planning on getting there. The more people spoke, the more I began to realize that they were not interested in understanding anxiety, solving the problem, or getting well. One lady talked about how she had agoraphobia, and that her mother had it, her daughter had it, and they all would get together at her house and talk about how bad their lives were. Another lady talked about her agoraphobia and how she tried to stay busy all the time in order to occupy her thoughts with something other than panic. She would work at home sewing quilts or knitting blankets. If she stopped for more than a few moments, she would get panicky. She never left the house except to come to this support group meeting. This had been going on for years. She had even brought her knitting supplies to the meeting and was knitting a blanket as she told the group her story.

More and more people shared their stories of a miserable existence. There was no talk of how to cope with it or heal. They all liked to talk about their medications and how long they had been living within the confines of their homes and work. I was the only one there with any glimmer of hope. One older gentleman told me that I'd better get used to it quick, because he'd been living with panic for twenty years, and that there was no getting over it. "It's always going to be there, and it only gets worse," he told me. They all ultimately told me that I would have to live with it. I spoke right up and let them know that I would not live with it. I was there looking for answers, trying to find someone who had been through my situation and returned to a normal life. I got a few funny looks and was told, "Good luck."

I wanted desperately to prove these people wrong. I told myself that once I was well, I was going to come back to this group and say "See, I told you I could do it!" In retrospect, I think they liked being part of a group so much that they didn't want to get well, that it was like a social gathering more than a recovery group. I thanked them for allowing me to visit, realizing that these were not the people to help me in my quest to get my life back. I needed a positive influence, and they were not going to provide that. I never attended another meeting.

On a side note, a few years after getting back to normal, I thought about paying the group a visit and giving a speech. As it turned out, the group dissolved a few months after my first visit. Who knows, maybe I inspired them all to change. I doubt it, but that raises a good point; you have to **want** to get well in order to get well, and you have to want it worse than you've ever wanted anything. You have to be determined to get your life back and let nothing stand in your way. It is not a quick or easy task. The easiest thing to do is give up and be like those folks at the support group meeting. The hardest thing to do is stick to your plan when things aren't going like you want or you don't see progress. Just remember that the rewards will be great if you stay the course. The opportunity to have your life back is there for the taking. The opportunities to give up seem to present themselves in direct proportion to how determined you are to succeed. The visit to the anxiety support group was my first opportunity to give up and accept the condition, just like the members of the group had done. As the saying goes, misery loves company. Determined not to give up that easily, I moved on to my next likely resource for help – my family doctor.

I went to see my family doctor in hopes of getting to the bottom of my condition. He came into the exam room accompanied by an intern and got my permission for the intern to observe. "Rafe, for the benefit of our intern, why don't you tell me what a panic attack is?" I went into my explanation of the physical symptoms and the accompanying mental symptoms. My doctor was impressed with my explanation and called it the "textbook definition" of a panic attack. The intern looked at me in disbelief. "What are you scared of? Dying? Is this like being stressed out over an exam?" He could not imagine someone getting in such a mental and physical state for apparently no reason. He had never had a panic attack or known of anyone who had experienced one. So I asked the question that had been pressing me, "How can I be fine one day and screwed up the next?" I got the "textbook answer" from them: "Oh, you just have a chemical imbalance in your brain. You're producing too much serotonin." They went on in doctor-speak for a few moments about the physical mechanisms that are at work during a panic attack. My next question was, "How can I suddenly have a chemical imbalance?" They danced around the question and could offer me no real answer. I was pressing them for an explanation of how this could happen seemingly overnight. I wanted to know how to fix the "chemical imbalance," if that was really what was wrong with me. They told me, essentially, that I couldn't fix it and were all too quick to write me a couple of prescriptions for anti-anxiety and anti-depressant pills. I let them know that I didn't want a pill to cover up the symptoms; I wanted to get to the root of the problem and correct it. I don't believe they were too used to a patient challenging them in this way. My doctor's words were "Rafe, it's 1998. We have a pill for that. The choice is simple: take the pill and feel better, or don't take the pill and be miserable. You decide."

So, my second attempt at getting some answers had led me again to someone who had accepted the condition. Only this time my doctor had accepted it for me, and just like the attitudes I found at the support group, he had decided that it was something that I should just accept. His answer was to pop pills to cover up the symptoms, just like those other people were doing. He offered me no alternative to medication or suggestions on how to get well. I stared at the prescriptions as he handed them to me, feeling discouraged, but not ready to give up just yet. Determined to get well without medication, my discouragement quickly turned into a deeper commitment to find answers and figure out how to get my life back.

On my way out of the doctor's office, I ran into a nurse practitioner. We had a brief conversation about why I was there and what I had been through. She showed a genuine interest in my situation as I expressed my determination to get well without medication. She recommended a psychologist that she had worked closely with and went on to explain how she had referred other patients with anxiety and panic issues to him. Alas, this trip had not been in vain. I had a lead! I was anxious to make contact with the psychologist and called him as soon as I got back home.

The day of our appointment had arrived, and I was anxiously awaiting the meeting. I had mixed feelings about seeing a psychologist. *Was this visit an admission of insanity?* I certainly wasn't going to tell anyone that I had seen him. They'd think I was crazy for sure. On the other hand, I was so desperate for answers and a plan to get well that I didn't care what anyone thought. I was also scared of what he might tell me. Maybe there was no way to get well. Maybe my only option was to take pills for the rest of my life. If this guy had never had a panic attack himself, how is he going to know what I'm going through?

Sherry drove me to the office and waited in the car while I went in for my meeting with the psychologist. We spent the first few minutes making small talk and getting to know each other. After that, I cut right to the chase. I asked if he'd ever experienced a panic attack first hand. He told me that he had not, but he knew what they felt like, according to other patients and what he had learned in his training. I expressed my desire to talk with someone that had been through my situation and had returned to normal. He seemed genuine about helping me, but he had never experienced panic first hand, so I couldn't put a lot of stock in taking advice from him. Would you rather take advice on bodybuilding from a 120 lb. weakling or Arnold Schwarzenegger? I wanted to talk to someone who had been through this and was well now, without being medicated.

He had me run in place the first session to show me that pounding in my chest didn't necessarily mean panic. We discussed my stress level prior to the panic attacks and concluded that stress was probably the cause of the panic attacks, but that I had developed agoraphobia, which is another anxiety disorder associated with panic. Well, at least I now had confirmation of the condition I was fighting. I asked about ways to overcome agoraphobia. We talked about the exposure technique, which I'll talk about later in this book. At the time, that sounded ridiculous. I asked for specific people that he had seen that had overcome panic and agoraphobia, but he could not provide names and numbers. I suppose I was asking a little too much. He did say that he knew people that had gotten well or were coping with it in one way or another. Some were dependent on pills, some weren't. I came away from the meeting with some reassurance that nothing was physically wrong with me and that somewhere someone had gotten over this; I just had to take his word for it.

I guess I got hung up on finding someone that had "been there, done that", so to speak. I felt so screwed up with all the physical symptoms and being such a mental wreck that I was desperate to find someone to fit that description. I knew that if I found such a person, I would have hope and inspiration. That person would tell me how they got well, and I could just copy his or her plan to get well myself. How can a psychologist tell me how to get well if he's never done it himself? Was he really any different than the doctor that wanted to prescribe pills? I wasn't really giving this guy a fair chance because I had made my mind up that the only person that could truly help me would have to have been through it. I halfheartedly went back to the psychologist for several more sessions because he was all I had to work with. I did pick up some valuable bits of information on panic and agoraphobia. I hadn't made any progress in the way of overcoming my fears of places or situations, but at least I was learning, so I felt like I was moving in the right direction.

In my quest to find someone who had been an agoraphobic and returned to a normal life, I made a few phone calls to people that I knew had experienced panic attacks. One was a woman that worked for my mother. Another was a woman that worked for my father-in-law. I got immediate sympathy from these women as I described what I was going through. Upon asking for information on their particular situations, I learned that each of them had varying degrees of agoraphobia themselves. They both had been living with fear and panic for years. Fear was always present in their daily lives. Both of these women were taking prescriptions for anxiety. One took them daily, and the other took them a few times a week as needed. One had resorted to working from home, and the other had to make excuses to leave work on a moment's notice and called in sick a lot. Both of these women knew other people with the same condition. One woman's daughter had it even worse than she, so I called her daughter also. She was nearly as bad off as I was but could still go to work. Her husband had to drive her everywhere, and she never did anything outside of her workplace or home. I got advice from these women, but it wasn't really the advice I was looking for. They were basically living with it, like the people in the support group. There was a difference in these women, however. They were all interested in getting well, but like me, didn't know how to go about it. A couple of them even asked me to call them back if I came across any good information on getting back to a normal life. They were more than willing to try anything. Here were three more people whom I would look forward to telling how I got well one day.

It seemed that the only people I could find were the ones who had submitted to the idea of living in fear or had decided to take the easy way out and become dependent on Xanax or Prozac for the rest of their lives. Why cover up the symptoms? I wanted to eliminate the cause, and then the symptoms would take care of themselves.

I finally came to the realization that I might not ever find anyone who had "been there, done that" by relying on my network of personal contacts. I couldn't let that hold me up any longer. I just had to have faith that someone had done it, maybe lots of people had, but I didn't have time to wait around to find them. I had to do this for myself and not rely on someone else to give me step-by-step instructions. If I was going to get well, I had to educate myself on my condition and then formulate a plan to get well. I decided that my first step would be to learn as much as I could about what was wrong with me.

I started reading anything I could get my hands on about panic and agoraphobia. Most materials were written by a doctor or psychiatrist who had never experienced it first hand, so I continued to have a hard time putting much stock in what they were telling me to do to get well, but I read on anyway. I bought book after book on panic and anxiety disorders - shopping online, of course, because the idea of going to a bookstore scared me. I figured that the more I understood about what causes panic, the better equipped I would be to overcome it. I learned about some of the common personality traits and disorders among agoraphobics, such as obsessive compulsive disorder (OCD), perfectionism, worrying about things that I had no control of, trying to please everyone, and being non-assertive. Yes, I had varying degrees of most of those personality traits, but I had had them all of my life; why are they just now catching up with me? (I now know the answer to that and will share it later.) The more I read, the more I realized that these characteristics were all self-defeating, stress-causing personality traits and that I possessed almost all of them.

I learned a lot about myself during this process. It was all finally starting to come together in the form of a plan now. I had gathered enough information to understand why I had my original panic attack and why it developed into agoraphobia. I could also identify both the internal and external forces that were at work that brought me to this place in my life. I had identified the things that I could change as well as the things over which I had no control. I finally knew what had to be done. This was an exciting revelation. I felt like a great military commander formulating a battle plan. I had to attack this situation on two fronts: handling panic, fear, and warding off panic attacks; and correcting my self-defeating, anxiety-producing personality traits.

## Deciding to Go for It

This was the turning point. I had wanted to get well for a while, but now I had an actual plan. So, I guess you can say I was recommitting to getting well. I really had no choice: I couldn't go on living the way I was. I refused to give in to fear. I refused to give in to drugs. The only thing left was to fight this and get better. I expected it to be difficult and didn't know how long it would take. The mere thought of facing fear was scary in itself. I was really faced with two choices: take action and try to get well, or take no action and keep living a miserable life.

# How I Got Well

## The Vision

The first step in my recovery plan was to develop a vision. We all wonder what it would be like to be like to reach a goal like wealth, fame, or thinness. When I was at my lowest, I used to wonder what it would be like to be normal again. I always daydreamed about it, but I never really believed it would happen. I had to develop a vision of myself being well. This time it was different. I had to believe that vision as if I knew it to be fact. I had to think of it as present tense. I had to see myself driving my car, going to the store, excelling in business, riding a roller coaster, giving a speech. Parts of this vision I developed were higher achievements than I had ever accomplished in my life.

I had committed to getting well and then created a vision of myself being well. This all sounded great. I didn't think

I would jump in the car on day one and take a road trip, but I did feel like it was time to start moving forward with my plan. You can probably guess what happened the first morning into my plan. That's right, I had a panic attack. I was so determined to get up and make a drastic change in my life that I believed I could just jump into a brand new routine. I wasn't ready for that. I put additional stress on myself by getting all pumped up to start something new, and it just sent me further into the grips of anxiety and fear.

Having the panic attack on day one of my new plan to get well sent me into despair. I began to doubt myself and thought that I was crazy for trying to get well on my own. *Just take the pills like everyone else and get on with your life*, I thought. Then I thought of everything I had been through, my commitment to myself and the desire to get well. I wanted it so bad. I gave myself a pep talk for the entire day: *It's okay if you fall off the horse today. Get back on. Tomorrow will be better. Even if it's not, you have the rest of your life to get well. Just keep making progress.*

Every time I had doubt or seemed to fall on my face, I let my vision fuel my determination. If you don't already know this fact, you will soon learn it: any time you set out to do something good, whether for yourself or someone else, you are going to be met with resistance. Once you realize that, you can expect resistance and include ways to overcome it in your plan. As a rule of thumb, the more good or noble your action or plan is, the more resistance you will meet. I can't imagine anything more worthwhile and rewarding than getting a life back. At that time in my life, the decision to get better was the most important I had ever made. Therefore, the resistance was coming at me in great force. To take it even deeper, I realized I had just emerged myself in an epic struggle of good versus evil. While most people just accept defeat, I had chosen to fight. When you look at it in those terms, you will open your eyes to just how many factors are working against you and begin to recognize them instantly. I began to regard panic and fear as a separate entity or being that I was destined to defeat in a great struggle. You need to think of things in those terms and really identify what you're up against here before you let resistance discourage you.

You WILL meet resistance. It will come in many forms, such as more panic attacks, doubt, fear, failure, depression, and hopelessness. Go ahead and plan on them. I will almost guarantee that you haven't seen your last panic attack. The fear of having another one will be your greatest resistance as you move forward. Don't give in. Let resistance be an indicator that you are doing the right thing.

## Overcoming Panic Attacks

In order to overcome or fend off panic attacks, I had to understand what a panic attack really is. In the simplest definition, a panic attack is your body's natural fight or flight response to a dangerous situation. This is something that is programmed into every human being on the planet. It is your body's built-in defense system, and the fact that you can have a panic attack is a good indicator that all the systems in your body are working correctly. If you are thrown in front of a speeding locomotive, your body has reason to go into this mode. Your heart rate and breathing elevate. Your mind knows there is a danger and that you must be superhuman long enough to get yourself to safety. This is a natural response to danger. The problem with panic sufferers is that their bodies go into this mode when there is no apparent reason for it to do so.

Panic attacks often start with a negative thought that triggers the body's built-in defense system. This is a very important point. I had come all this way thinking that panic attacks started with a flutter in my chest or shortness of breath. In my research, I read that it has been believed to be triggered by a negative or troubling thought. This made perfect sense to me. Now I realized that panic attacks really don't come out of nowhere; they are born in that fleeting negative thought, no matter how insignificant. Once I had learned of this, I started to take note every time I felt the onset of panic. Sure enough, I almost always had a negative thought a moment before the physical onset. These negative thoughts that triggered panic could be something as trivial as a thought about my job or doing anything that caused me stress, like waiting in a line or dealing with a difficult person. Sometimes I had to really think about why a certain thought triggered panic because it seemed so insignificant.

The negative thought may create a weak or strong physical sensation relative to how troubling the thought is. It could be something as mild as a flutter in the chest or as strong as severe chest pains. Your reaction to the physical sensation could be just as varied. Your mental response could be anything from *That's nothing to be concerned with* to *Oh no, I'm having a heart attack*, and that reaction generates more negative thoughts and fear, which spawn further physical sensation. You may feel tightness in your chest, shortness of breath, numbness or tingling in your extremities, dizziness, or a variety of other physical sensations. These physical symptoms are those often associated with a heart attack, which creates even stronger negative thoughts, and so on. To put it simply, they scare the hell out of you. The next thing you know, you've spiraled into a full-blown panic attack from merely thinking about your mother-in-law coming over. This cycle of events can happen in a matter of a few moments in some cases or build up over the course of several minutes. The key to managing panic is to not let yourself spiral out of control and get to the point of a full-blown panic attack. I eventually learned to manage this cycle to the point of stopping a panic attack dead in its tracks. Now I know without a doubt that I'll never have another one.

## My Panic First Aid Kit

My control of panic attacks didn't happen overnight. The first thing I did to help manage panic was to try to eliminate the negative thoughts that triggered even the slightest physical sensation. That's easier said than done, but with a little practice and self-awareness, you'll catch yourself dwelling on a negative thought and learn to quickly flush it out of your mind and replace it with a positive thought, all the while being aware of your body's physical state. Eventually, I learned to shrug off the flutters associated with the negative thought and never let it progress to the point of panic onset. Sometimes early on, this was not so easy to do, so the next step in handling panic was to develop a Panic First Aid Kit.

The first item in my kit was my deep breathing exercise. Most panic sufferers are shallow breathers. By shallow breathing I mean breathing from the upper part of your chest. Chances are that if you're a panic sufferer or live in a state of heightened anxiety, you breathe shallow all the time. Shallow breathing causes a deficiency in oxygen to your blood. This problem is compounded during a panic attack as your breathing becomes faster, therefore causing the numbness and tingling sensations associated with hyperventilation. So it stands to reason that if you are a habitual shallow breather, you already have one strike against you in the fight against panic.

The following deep breathing exercise became part of my daily routine; whether I was panicky or not, I often checked on my breathing pattern and would perform this exercise any time I noticed that I was shallow breathing. My reasoning here is that I wanted to eliminate anything working against me that might contribute to panic. The great thing about this exercise is that you can do it anywhere, and it only takes a couple of minutes. The effects are felt almost instantly. It is best to do this breathing exercise any time you become anxious and not wait for the onset of panic before you pull this one out of the bag. Since this breathing technique triggers part of the nervous system that helps you relax, it was particularly helpful in getting to sleep at night. I often did this exercise while lying in bed at night and would usually go right to sleep shortly afterwards.

1. Slowly exhale all the air from your lungs through your mouth.
2. Take a deep abdominal breath through the nose while counting to eight, filling the lungs. Be sure you are breathing from your lower abdomen. Rest your hands just below your belly button and feel your abdomen pushing your hands outward as you breathe from the gut.
3. Hold your breath while counting to eight again.
4. Exhale through the mouth while counting to eight.
5. Repeat two more times.

The other part of this exercise involves cleansing your mind of negative thoughts. Not only is this a physical exercise but a mental exercise as well. This will help you stabilize yourself physically while getting your mind where it should be. As you exhale, feel yourself blowing out all the negative thoughts that are in your mind. Take a negative thought such as *Something is wrong with me* and blow it away. Flush it from your thoughts. As you inhale, replace that negative thought with a positive thought or one of the verbal affirmations below like *I'm totally healthy.*

*The doctors have told me so.* It is very important that you focus on replacing negative thoughts with positive ones while you do this exercise, especially if you are in the pre-stages of a panic attack. Otherwise, you free your mind up to focus on the physical sensations or panicky thoughts that contribute to the spiraling that ultimately leads to a panic attack.

The next item in my Panic First Aid Kit was a list of positive affirmations that I read out loud whenever I felt a panic attack coming on. These affirmations helped during the onset of panic to keep me from spiraling into a panic attack. I could go from chest pains to full-blown attack in a matter of three minutes or less once the spiraling started. These affirmations were a vital tool in helping me control the spiraling and neutralize the fear.

1.  I am the same person right now as I am when I'm in my safe zone. (I would visualize myself in my safe zone and feel the calmness that place brought to me.)
2.  I am not having a heart attack.
3.  I am perfectly healthy. The doctors have told me so.
4.  I am not going to die from this.
5.  I am in control of my body and my thoughts.
6.  I am calm.
7.  I am at peace.

I wrote these on a note card and carried the card with me. I had them all memorized, but there was something about seeing them on paper and reading them out loud that made them seem more real to me. I listed these affirmations in order according to how strongly they rang with me. The first one was always a slap in the face to me when I needed it: *I am the same person right now as I am when I'm in my safe zone.* Put this book down right now and think about that statement for a few minutes. You are the same person no matter where you are. I always talked to myself on this one. What reason is there for being scared at the store or in the car? You are the same physical person everywhere you go. Unless you are being thrown from an airplane, you shouldn't feel like you're about to die. Every time I got panicky, I read that affirmation and asked myself, *Would I be panicky this very moment if I were at home? Of course not. So why am I panicky now? Am I in danger?* The answer was always *No.*

My cell phone was another item in my first aid kit. I knew that no matter where I was, I could call for help if I needed it. Sometimes just calling my wife and talking about anything would get my mind off panic. I called her from the car a lot and sometimes kept her on the phone until I got to where I was going. It kept my mind occupied during times of high anxiety and was a great way to get through a bad day of traffic.

The last item in my kit was Xanax. For the first few months of recovery, I kept a single Xanax pill in my pocket all the time. I also had them stashed away in various places like the car and my desk drawer at work. I knew that if all else failed, I could take one of these and feel better almost immediately. Xanax was my last resort because I knew it came with consequences. The relief would only be temporary, a day or two at best. Then I had to go through the rebound stages as the drug wore off. This meant that I would feel worse than I did before taking the pill. That was something that I wasn't necessarily willing to endure. I knew that it would only take one or two pills for me to get roped into an addiction to Xanax. I didn't want to have that dependency on them. The pill in my pocket was kind of like my emergency parachute; I knew I could use it if everything else failed.

This Panic First Aid Kit is what I used to fight off panic attacks for the first few months of overcoming panic attacks and agoraphobia. At first, I relied on the affirmations and breathing exercise almost daily. Over time I relied on these things less and less. I eventually did away with the note cards and stopped carrying the Xanax pills with me.

## Don't Dwell on Fear

My first thought every day was *How do I feel?* I continually dwelled on my physical state. I thought about my condition constantly. I knew I had to stop waking up every day anticipating anxiety. I felt good in the mornings for the first half hour or so while I waited for the nervousness to turn on as I reminded myself that I had a problem. Then it was like a light switch coming on: my body went into a different physical state. I went through a hoard of physical anxiety symptoms, and once the switch was on, I felt anxious all day. This feeling made it hard for me to leave my safe zone because I felt like I was already on the verge of panic. This pattern improved over time as I started to have a goal each day to focus my thoughts on. I eventually broke the habit of waking up in anticipation of feeling bad by replacing those thoughts with my goals for the day.

## The Stress Bucket

Now we are at the core of the original panic problem, so pay attention to this part in particular. Remember how all these problems with panic and anxiety seemed to come out of nowhere? They didn't. Your stress bucket got full, and one extra drop sent you spilling over the edge, just like the straw that broke the camel's back. Once you understand the concept of your stress bucket, you are on your way to mastering the final, and possibly the most important, piece of the puzzle in getting and staying well.

Every human being on earth has his or her own unique threshold for stress. We'll call it the stress bucket. Think of it as what you use to carry your stress in. You might have a five-gallon stress bucket, I might have a three-gallon stress bucket, and your neighbor might have a ten-gallon bucket. So we're all walking around with different capacities for stress. You are constantly filling and emptying your bucket. You never empty your bucket completely. There are normal everyday stressors that should be going in and out of your bucket constantly. Things like having to go to work, pick up kids from school, and preparing dinner for the family are normal, everyday stressors. That kind of stress is for the most part healthy and should never by itself come anywhere near filling your bucket.

Other types of stress are not so healthy. These are the stressors that take up large amounts of room in your bucket, leaving very little space for those normal kinds of stressors to fit in. As your bucket approaches the full mark, you might start to feel anxious, nervous, irritable, or stressed out. Some people may feel almost nothing at all. Living with an almost full stress bucket may be a normal state of being for you, but it will eventually catch up with you. Once your bucket is completely full and that final drop of stress enters the bucket, you have exceeded your stress threshold, and for people like me and you, that's what triggers a panic attack.

Overfilling my stress bucket is what triggered my first panic attack and most likely yours, too. In my opinion, this is the real story behind the so called "chemical imbalance" that my doctor was so quick to diagnose. The chemical imbalance was nothing more than an overflowing stress bucket. That was the real problem. My bucket was brimming just before my first panic attack, and I didn't even realize it. I felt fine, but I had no idea that I had reached my personal limit of stress and that I was going around with not one drop of room to spare in my bucket. The one drop that sent me over the edge was that fleeting negative thought I had while driving in my car. Since I had absolutely no room left for stress, that single, almost insignificant thought about my job created just enough of a stressful association in me that it was the drop that sent my bucket spilling over. That's how my first panic attack seemed to come out of nowhere.

The reality was that I had completely filled my bucket and had exceeded my threshold. So, the obvious question now is this: what fills my stress bucket? The answer is external and internal stressors. I had to figure out what was filling mine, just as you will figure out what is filling yours. Let's start with the things that are the biggest fillers of stress buckets - Top Life Stressors. These would qualify as external stressors. Here are the main life stressors in no particular order:

## Top Life Stressors

Death of a family member or someone close to you

Getting married

Divorce or separation

New job or promotion

Moving/buying or selling your home

Becoming a new parent

Losing your job

Change in financial status

Final exams/graduation from college

Being separated from spouse or family

The top life stressors take up massive amounts of room in your stress bucket and therefore leave little room for much else. Again, it all depends on your personal capacity.

We all handle these life stressors differently. Play along with me for a moment. Let's say that I have a five-gallon bucket and you have a ten-gallon bucket. Let's also say that getting married takes up four gallons for both of us. Now your bucket is 40% full. My bucket is 80% full. You've got plenty of room left in your bucket, but I have only 20% left now. You could also say that we have the same size buckets, and that marriage takes up different amounts for each of us. The point is that these top life stressors take up vast amounts of room in your bucket. The top life stressors not only take up lots of room, but these types of stressors take a long time to get emptied from your bucket. A death in the family might keep your bucket at 50% for a year after the event. Three years later, the stress from that event may still be occupying 30% of your bucket. The more major life stressors that you have experienced in a short period of time, the more likely that they are piled up in your bucket taking up lots of space.

When I had my first panic attack, I had been through three of these top life stressors within a relatively short period of time. I was a newlywed, was on a new job in which I had been promoted quickly, and had just moved. Just one of these events would be enough to take up 30% or 40% of my bucket. I had three of these things piled up in my stress bucket! Add the stress of building computers on the side, putting a wife through college, being the sole breadwinner, and living with all of my internal stressors, and it's no wonder that I ended up in the emergency room with a panic attack.

Now that you know about the top life stressors, it stands to reason that most people with anxiety disorder, panic attacks, and agoraphobia are in their early 20s to early 30s. This is the age range when these top life stressors typically take place in a person's life. Your career is taking off. You get married. You buy a house. You decide to have children. For others, you may be going through your first divorce or dealing with the death of a parent. This is the time when your life seems to be the most eventful and exciting. For me, it was most certainly the combination of these major life events and some other identified stressors that had my stress bucket completely full. I simply exceeded my limit for stress.

So, what about those stressors? How do I get them out of my bucket? That was my first question. It's not an easy one to answer. The first thing to do is identify them and realize that they are occupying space in your bucket. I realized that I had three of them piled up on top of each other. For me, just knowing what caused all of this in the first place gave me a sense of relief that freed up some room in my bucket. I actually spent some time reflecting on these events. I took each one at a time and thought about the positive and negative associations with each. Moving, for example, had caused me much stress. I meditated on that event, thinking about the entire process and how it affected me. I thought about everything from renting the moving truck to packing and unloading the truck and living out of boxes for weeks. I thought about how tired and disoriented moving left me feeling. Then I visualized this event occupying space in my bucket. I had to tell myself that the event was over. I didn't need to think anymore about that event. I visualized myself pouring this event out of my bucket.

The techniques for recognizing the stress of marriage, the new job, and the promotion were a little different, mostly because in my mind they were pleasurable events. I still took time to acknowledge that they were factors in my stress overload and visualized pouring them out of my bucket. I did all this knowing that they were still going to occupy space in my stress bucket for a while, but hopefully this would make them smaller and speed up the process.

All of these top life stressors are what I call external stress. These are events that take place in your life that are sometimes out of your control, like a death in the family or losing your job. Sometimes they are a result of your own actions, like getting married or receiving a promotion. For the most part, they are unavoidable events in the sense that they are just part of life. These external stressors occupy space in your stress bucket and may stay in there for long periods of time. Identifying my own external stressors and acknowledging that they occupied space in my stress bucket was the first step in emptying my bucket. I took time to reflect on each of the events and then mentally let go of them.

The other type of stress that can fill your bucket is what I call internal stress. Internal stress is a result of how you interact with people, how you react to events, and simply how you handle stress. The good news about internal stressors is that they can move in and out of your stress bucket quickly. This means that if your bucket is mostly full of internal stressors, you can take action immediately to get them out of your stress bucket. Taking these actions to correct or eliminate internal stressors for me meant having to make some major changes in my personality and character.

I realized that I had a few major "personality flaws" that were the cause of almost all of my internal stress. First of all, I was the most non-assertive person that you would ever meet. Let me give you some examples of my non-assertiveness. I avoided conflict at any cost; if I went to a restaurant and ordered a hamburger, and the waitress brought out a salad by mistake, I just ate it and said nothing to her about the mistake. If she happened to notice that she made an error, I might have said "Oh, that's ok, I'll eat it. It's really no problem." I just took on the totally avoidable stress of having to eat something I didn't like because I didn't want to assert myself enough to tell the waitress that she messed up my order. That's internal stress in my bucket. I remember as a kid being the one that was bullied all the time, and I never stood up for myself. I got a brand new bicycle once, and a neighbor kid asked to ride it. Of course I didn't want him to ride it, but I couldn't tell him "No." He wrecked it. He returned it to me with scratches and dirt all over it, I said nothing. I had to live with the stress and disappointment of having a brand new bike that was all messed up now because I didn't tell the kid "No, I don't want you riding my new bike."

Even as an adult, I was never able to say "No" to people for fear of making them angry or hurting their feelings. It was always at the expense of my own feelings and my own stress. I let people walk all over me. That type of non-assertive behavior followed me through life all the way up until the day I decided that I couldn't be that way any more if I wanted to get well. Once I identified my non-assertiveness as a source of internal stress, I knew that I had to change it immediately. I realized that the five seconds of saying "No" or standing up for myself was a whole lot better than the days or weeks of stress for having said "Yes" or not standing up for myself. I could easily identify several things taking up space in my stress bucket that could have been avoided if I had just said "No" to a few people. Would it have made them mad? Probably not. Would they still like me? Probably so. I had to tell myself that saying "Yes" to everyone at the expense of my own health and well-being was not worth it. Becoming assertive was not something that I could just ease into. I didn't have time for that. My health and wellness hinged on making these life changes. The only way for me to make a change like this was to go at it with an all-or-nothing attitude. This was going to be awkward at first, but I was prepared to endure the first few times in order to get over the hurdle. Once I made a decision to be assertive, I turned it on like a light switch. It was the most empowering feeling I had ever experienced. I put it into practice immediately, and I felt instant relief.

The next thing that I recognized as an internal stressor was my relentless pursuit of perfectionism. Everything I did had to be perfect, and I went to all lengths to make it so. For example, in college I had to be part of several group projects. The instructor would break the class into groups of students, and each student was graded on the performance of the group as a whole. I always ended up doing everyone's job in the group because the project had my name on it, and I wanted the best grade. No one could do anything to my satisfaction, so I always volunteered to help everyone. Now, being non-assertive made this a little difficult because I couldn't just come right out and say "I don't like the way you're doing that." My way around it was often just volunteering to do another person's work on top of my own.

Perfectionism stayed with me throughout my life. It carried over into my job. My goal was always to show everyone up. I never did anything that was just simply satisfactory; it had to be heads above the rest. If I was writing software, it had to have more bells and whistles than expected. Everything I did had to be completely flawless. I toiled over minute details that no one else but me would ever notice. Here again was another example of internal stress in my bucket that was self-inflicted. I had to start accepting "good" as good enough. If something turned out perfect, then that was great, but I would no longer work myself up over getting it perfect. If my clients were happy, then there was no need to keep improving on something that they already liked.

Perfectionism was one of the hardest things for me to let go of. One of the ways out of it was to ask if beating myself up over a minute detail that no one would notice or even care about was worth the price of my health. Of course it's not. Good is good. Perfect the first time is a bonus. I left it at that.

Obsessive Compulsive Disorder (OCD) is a common disorder among panic and agoraphobia sufferers. I'm not going to go into depth on the subject; there are lots of books on it if you're interested in learning more. There are varying degrees of OCD, and I believe that certain behaviors classified as OCD are traits found in most people. Checking locked doors is one example. I read about people with OCD who couldn't drive through an intersection without turning around to see if they had caused an accident. Others are obsessed with germs and wash their hands too frequently. Others like to organize or clean to a meticulous extent. I, on the other hand, was basically a slob when it came to keeping things around the house tidy, but I did have some behaviors that I considered borderline OCD. I was a lock checker: I checked the doors three or four times before going to bed at night. I was a hand washer: I washed my hands after going out in public. I liked to put objects in straight lines and organize in a symmetrical manner. I didn't really consider these behaviors as bad, but I flushed them before they got any worse. I learned to check a door once, tell myself, *It's locked. Don't check it again*, and forget it. Even though very minor, those OCD behaviors were adding stress to my bucket, and they had to go. If you think that you are suffering from OCD, take steps to get help. That's just more stress in your bucket that you don't need if you're going to stay well.

Learning to say "No" was the next new skill that I had to acquire – not in the sense of being assertive necessarily, but rather saying no to myself as well. I was an overachiever who was having a hard time really achieving anything. I tried to take on more than I could handle. The problem became that I was not getting anything done for trying to do too many things at once. Some things were either not getting done at all or getting poorly done. For a perfectionist, that made it even harder on me. I took on responsibilities, one after another. I think the reasons I took on so much were that I wanted to make everyone happy, wanted the recognition, or simply wanted the sense of accomplishment. I seemed to be making more and more commitments that I couldn't keep. Now, you can bet that as an agoraphobic I was no longer in a commitment crisis. I could still barely leave the house, but I identified this behavior as a source of stress that was a big factor in what led me to panic originally. I was going to be sure that once I got back on my feet, I would not over-commit myself again. That is another example of avoidable stress that I needed to eliminate, or should I say prevent.

Repeat after me: "So what?" Say it again out loud. Shout it. "SO WHAT?" Those two words became my motto. I lived by these words for a long time. I had to. If you are serious about overcoming panic, you've got to turn all of your "what if's" into "so what's." Don't let the "what if's" stop you from getting well. I had to let go of all worry. Worry was adding stress to my bucket. When you absolutely get fed up with living a life ruled by fear, it becomes very easy to take on the "so what" attitude.

The day I decided to step out of my comfort zone and walk to the mailbox at the end of the driveway was the first time I said "So what?" It wasn't automatic. At first I stood there thinking about all the "what if's." *What if I have a panic attack? What if I have a heart attack and die? What if I can't do it?* I had to get fed up enough to say "so what?" If taking that walk was going to kill me, then so what? I wasn't living anyway. What was the worst thing that could have happened by walking to the mailbox? Another panic attack? So what? It wasn't the first one and probably wouldn't be the last. It was absolutely imperative that I stopped worrying. Worry was one of the biggest internal stressors filling my bucket at the time of my first panic attack. I worried about everything. *Is that person mad at me? What do people think of me? Am I ever going to be a success at anything? How will I ever catch up on all of my bills? What if I can't find a good job? What if something happens to my parents? Who will take care of their business? Who will take care of my brother?* I even made up things to worry about. I had to flush all worry by taking on a "So what?" attitude. Don't confuse worry with care. I still cared about things.

I just decided not to worry about so many things, especially things over which I had no control. If you're not crippled by panic or have not reached the point of being fed up with a miserable life, what you're about to read will probably sound unreasonable, unacceptable or irresponsible. If you are fed up like I was, then what I'm going to say next is going to be a liberating force and giant step towards getting well. I had to say "So what?" to my worries, including debt worries. Keep in mind that I did not own a home at the time, so I'm not suggesting that you stop paying your mortgage. I also want to make it clear that I did not file bankruptcy or let my debts go unpaid. I did, however, fall way behind on many financial obligations as a result of not being able to work. The point I'm trying to make here is that my natural tendency was to let these burdens of debt weigh on me and fill my bucket. I could not allow these things into my bucket. I did not stop *caring* about debt; I simply stopped *worrying* about the debt. If my credit was ruined, "So what?" As an agoraphobic, I couldn't work enough at the time to pay everyone, so it was going to happen anyway. Why worry? So what if my credit got ruined? It was worth the price of getting well to me. I had the rest of my life to rebuild my credit. Like I mentioned, I did care about it. I simply contacted everyone to whom I owed money and explained that I was unable to make the payments at the time. They all worked with me. They all eventually got paid. I was able to buy a house and three cars a few years later with no hassles. In the end, it all ended up being okay. That's the way it is with most worries. You have to ask yourself if worrying about something is worth the price of your good health. Is it worth the price of you not being able to drive to the mall or attend your son's graduation? Is worry worth missing your daughter's first dance recital? Is worry worth losing your job and never meeting your career goals? Is worry worth never having another romantic evening with your spouse because you can't leave the house? It wasn't for me, and I've got a good feeling that if you're reading this book right now, the only thing important for you is getting your life back, no matter what you have to do. So decide right now to stop worrying and pour those things out of your stress bucket.

Here is a great exercise that I did to alleviate worry. This is a good way to get that stress bucket emptied quickly. Write down everything on your mind. Make a list of everything that's bothering you, worrying you, or causing you stress. My list included everything from needing to pick up dry cleaning to the car payment that was overdue. I got everything I could think of out of my head and onto that paper. This paper became my worry list. I decided that I was not going to carry these things around with me anymore. They were going to stay on the paper and not in my head. If they were not in my head, then they were not in my stress bucket. I also decided that I would designate a time to visit this worry list. At that time, I would address things on the list and take any actions necessary to get them off my list. Once my time with the worry list was up, I was to leave the worries on the paper and not take them with me. Once I got everything out of my head and onto paper, I separated the items into two columns. In the first column, I put all the items that I had absolutely no control over. I then read each one out loud, said to myself "I'm flushing this," and then crossed it off the list. There is simply no reason to worry about something you cannot control. There are some things you might want to prepare for. It might be worthwhile to make preparations for a worst-case scenario. If that's the case, move the preparations to the other list, those items you can control. Now it becomes a to-do item instead of a worry. So, the second column is the column of things you do have control over. I rewrote this column in order of priority. Then it was a matter of taking the allocated time every day to visit the worry list and attack the items one at a time until they had all been dealt with. Just having everything down on paper made it easy for me to mentally flush them all. I didn't feel like I had to walk around trying to remember everything there was to worry about. I also knew that I did not have to worry about those things constantly. There was a designated time to "worry," which really turned into time for taking action and resolving things in an orderly fashion without all the stress in my bucket of worrying about everything at once and getting nothing done.

I'm going to throw one last item into the mix of internal stressors before we move on. This applies to agoraphobics. Worrying about your next panic attack and letting fear control your actions is a stressor big enough to keep your bucket full all by itself! You may have a bucket that is at a moderate level when you're in your safe zone. As soon as you leave your safe zone, the fear of having a panic attack instantly fills your bucket. That means that you're out there with only a drop or two of stress capacity left in your bucket. You're constantly on the verge of panic. That is why it's important to overcome your fear of panic attacks themselves and your fear of leaving your safe zone. These two go hand in hand and are the biggest internal stressors you can have. Overcoming the fear will free up much needed space in your stress bucket.

As you know, my safe zone had diminished to the house and yard. I identified the fear of leaving my safe zone, and ultimately having another panic attack, as my biggest internal stressor. As with internal stressors, it could move in and out of my bucket quickly. It filled my stress bucket as soon as I left my safe zone. It poured out of my stress bucket as soon as I returned to my safe zone. I had to change the way leaving my safe zone affected my stress bucket. My plan was to lessen the impact by mastering control of panic attacks through the use of my panic first aid kit and to expand my safe zones through what is known as the exposure technique, which you will learn about later. I want to take a moment to recap the cause of panic and my course of action.

I had finally uncovered the truth about why I had suddenly been overcome with panic attacks and quickly turned into an agoraphobic. That truth was this: everyone has a unique capacity for stress, called a stress bucket. A combination of recent major life events and my own personal stress-causing attributes contributed to filling my stress bucket. Once my stress bucket became full, one drop of stress sent my bucket spilling over, resulting in my first panic attack. The fear of having another panic attack was so great that I quickly developed agoraphobia. My life was ruled by fear. I developed a plan of action to overcome panic and agoraphobia without drugs and maintain a normal lifestyle not ruled by fear. My plan was to fight this battle on two fronts: overcoming panic and agoraphobia and emptying my stress bucket so that I was no longer susceptible to panic. I overcame panic attacks by creating my own panic first aid kit and employing the tools in the kit anytime I felt panic coming on. I went to work on emptying my stress bucket by identifying the things that were filling my stress bucket and addressing them. Some things would take time to be emptied from my bucket, and others could be emptied immediately. The last part of my plan was to overcome agoraphobia, which for me went hand in hand with panic. I used goal setting along with the exposure technique (discussed later) to overcome agoraphobia and the panicky situations that came along with getting outside my safe zones.

## Setting Goals: Getting Out of My Safe Zone

All of this self discovery about my stress bucket was very eye opening. I had decided to make some major changes in myself and implement them right away. I had also developed this panic first aid kit that would help me get through or prevent panic attacks at the onset. Now only one thing was missing – leaving my safe zone so I could use all these new tools. After all, I only felt panicky when I left my safe zone; I didn't need all this newfound knowledge if I planned to keep sitting around the house. As I mentioned earlier, I had a panic attack on the first day I decided to make a change in my life. The problem was that I thought I could just jump out of my safe zone. Well, this takes a little time. I had to regroup and make a plan for getting out of my safe zone. This was as big a part of the process as mastering panic attacks themselves and emptying my stress bucket.

*What would I like to be able to do a month from now? Six months from now? A year from now? What is the ultimate goal that will let me know without a doubt that I am well?* These were goal questions that I had to keep me pushing forward. These goals all involved leaving my safe zone. I cannot stress enough how important it was to have goals to get me through and keep me focused. Setting short-term and long-term goals gave me a reason to get up in the morning and move forward with getting my life back. I could also feel a sense of accomplishment quickly by establishing some short term goals. I created a short-term goal of being able to drive to the grocery store, go inside, pick up something, stand in line, pay for it, and drive myself home. I would work towards larger goals by having smaller daily goals that led up to the larger goal. Driving around the block might be the first smaller goal that builds up to driving to the store. I created a long-term goal of being able to go out to a crowded restaurant and stay for the whole meal. Another long term goal was to take a vacation. I wanted to be able to fly or drive on a long trip somewhere far away from my safe zone.

I accomplished all of these goals and more. I did things that I would have never even attempted before panic. There was one goal that I set that I thought would let me know without a doubt that I was completely recovered from panic and agoraphobia. That goal was to fly to Disney World in Orlando, Florida and ride on Space Mountain. In May 2000 I did just that. My wife and I flew down for our 10th anniversary, and I not only rode

Space Mountain: I rode almost every single ride in Magic Kingdom, Epcot, Animal Kingdom, and MGM Studios. I even rode the Tower of Terror, which has an elevator that drops you 13 floors in the dark! I cannot explain the sense of accomplishment that I felt when I got off that ride. I was on top of the world, grinning from ear to ear. My wife and I rode it together. When we got off the ride, she looked at me and said, "Rafe, you are well!" I didn't have to say a thing. I just smiled and looked back at her, and we both knew that panic would never be a part of my life again.

Later in life, I have gone on to accomplish things that I would have never even considered before my life-changing bout with panic. I look for challenges and am constantly in pursuit of self improvement. I started a company and took on the role of sales manager. This requires me to be very assertive. I have done everything from make cold calls on the phone to approach complete strangers in hopes of making a good business contact. I joined BNI, a business group that requires me to speak every week for one minute regarding my business and our services. The thought of speaking to the BNI group intimidated me tremendously at first. In fact, most people fear public speaking almost as much as they fear death. I learned about Toastmasters, an organization that teaches effective public speaking. I joined

Toastmasters originally to overcome my fear of speaking for one minute each week to my BNI group. I became so confident in public speaking that I decided to accept the nomination of president of the BNI group. I served four consecutive terms as president and am currently serving as a trainer. These duties require me to conduct group training sessions and serve as a guest speaker at various events. I also joined my local chamber of commerce and have been active as a volunteer as well as chairing several committees. I have played in a band and have performed in front of thousands of people. Amazingly, I performed solo for nine thousand people on one occasion. I also performed for the governor's inaugural ball. These are just a few examples of how I overcame fear to have a better life. When I was curled up in a ball in my in-laws' spare bedroom scared to leave the house, I would have never believed any of those things possible in a million years. Don't limit your goals to just being able to drive and go shopping. Think of all the possibilities for your life and raise the bar. Let those visions be your guide.

## Achieving My Goals: The Exposure Technique

So how did I accomplish all these goals that involved expanding my safe zone? I used a technique that doctors call the exposure technique, and it involves, in a phased approach, desensitizing yourself to places or situations that you have associated with panic attacks. Most panic sufferers or agoraphobics will avoid the place or situation where they had their first panic attack because they have associated that place or situation with panic. It's as if you think that returning to that place will invoke a panic attack. I had my first panic attack in a shopping mall food court. Once my panic disorder had kicked in and turned to agoraphobia, I was terrified of malls and restaurants. I also avoided supermarkets and most other places where there were lots of people, especially if standing in line was involved. I had to expand my safe zones to include these places that I had come to avoid. Ultimately, safe zones would be a thing of the past. The whole world would become my safe zone.

Some people have many safe zones. I had a single safe zone. As you may recall, my safe zone had diminished to include my in-laws' house and yard. With such a limited zone, I had my work cut out for me. The first few minutes after waking up every morning were critical for me and could shape my mental state for the whole day. First of all, it was extremely important to get out of the habit of waking up each day and asking myself how I felt. I seemed to anticipate the nervousness and heavy burdened feeling of anxiety. If you wake up every day expecting to feel bad, then you will. I had to eliminate that thought process by replacing it with something positive and constructive. I needed something else to occupy my thoughts. So, every night before going to sleep, I set a goal for the next day. These goals were small daily goals that would get me closer to reaching a short term "exposure" goal like going to the store. Before going to sleep the night before, I visualized myself achieving my goal for the next day. My first thought in the morning was another visualization of me achieving the goal. As time went by, that onset of nervousness came later and later. Having a goal every day to think about kept me from reminding myself that I had panic disorder, and therefore kept that awful, sick, depressing, nervous, anxious feeling away. Some of you will know what I'm talking about. It's hard to describe this thing you drag around with you that seems to settle in every day. It's like a separate entity that invades your mind and body just after waking up and reminds you of your panic problem. I'm here to tell you that it goes away. Having a goal every day kept that panic monster away from me.

One of the first short-terms goals for me was to be comfortable driving again. Once I was comfortable driving, I could then work on my next goal of going shopping at the grocery store. Driving was going to be required to achieve most of my goals because all my goals involved leaving the house. I already knew that I couldn't just jump behind the wheel and drive down the road. I needed to take baby steps. My first daily goal was to get in the car by myself, start the engine, and back down the driveway. I visualized it the night before. I woke up that morning and visualized doing it with no problems. I got in the car, started it up, and backed down the driveway. Once I reached the end of the driveway, I sat there until I felt comfortable. Once I felt comfortable, I set the goal for the next day – I would drive around the block. I had achieved my goal for the day! Now what do I do? Here's where I made my first mistake. This is also what prolonged getting well for me. After achieving my daily goal, usually first thing in the morning, I crawled right back into my safe zone until the next day. Guess what happened to me once I had stopped thinking about the goals? You guessed it: the panic returned. I didn't have full-blown panic attacks, but that heavy, oppressing feeling would settle in around the middle of the day. This happened because I didn't have anything else to do, and I returned to dwelling on my condition. The next positive time of goal planning and visualization wouldn't come until later that night. That left the rest of the day open for me to think about my condition. I had to stop returning to thinking about my anxiety problem when there was nothing else to think about. I learned to have other things to do each day after I had worked on my exposure goals; and once I figured that out, healing came more quickly and more smoothly.

I could now drive my car around the block. That really wasn't a big deal for me. The next step was driving a mile or so to the grocery store. That was going to be a little bit more of a challenge because traffic lights were involved. I hated sitting at red lights, so that would be something else for me to overcome. I visualized driving there and feeling comfortable doing it. I got up the next morning, visualized it again, and then got in the car. I drove to the store and parked with no problems. I had mild anxiety at times but was very much in control. I parked the car there and sat for a while, watching the people go in and out. I set a goal of going in and buying something the next day. As I watched these people go in and out, I thought, *See, they aren't scared. There is nothing in that store that should cause me to panic. I'm the same person at home and right here in the car. I'll be the same person in that store tomorrow.* The next day, I drove to the store and went inside. The following day, I stood in line and bought something. The day after that, I stayed in the store for a while before checking out. I took this same approach to expanding my safe zone to include going out to eat, going to the mall, and anything else I wanted to be able to do. I took it slowly and stayed just outside my safe zone all the time. It did not happen overnight.

I noticed that if I didn't get out of the house for a day, it was harder to go out the next time. It's very tempting to slip back into your comfort zone and hibernate. I compare it to dieting and bodybuilding. If you cheat on your diet for a day, the next day you crave more junk food. You start sliding back into your old habits of eating poorly and before you know it, you're off the diet and you've gained all your weight back plus some. Getting back into the routine becomes more difficult every time you cheat. If you skip going out of the house and leaving your safe zone for a day, the next day makes it even more challenging. You're tempted to take another day off and curl up in front of the television. A few days of this in a row, and you're going to feel like you're starting all over again because you've lost your strength. With the exposure technique, you're conditioning yourself to withstand exposure much like a bodybuilder conditions his muscles to perform the task of lifting weights. Working out on a regular basis keeps the bodybuilder conditioned to lift heavy weights every day. By working out every day, not only is he as strong as he was the day before, but he gets a little stronger every day. If the bodybuilder takes a few days off, it takes him several days to get back to where he was because his body has lost some of its strength. Leaving my safe zone every day was like building a muscle. I added a little more strength every day by doing just a little more than I did the day before. I stayed just outside my comfort zone long enough to condition myself to each situation or place. Over time, my safe zones got larger and my level of anxiety (resistance to exposure) got smaller. Eventually, I built up my exposure muscles enough that every place became my safe zone. Once I conditioned myself to that level, safe zones became a thing of the past. I went anywhere and did anything without a second thought.

## Setbacks

The road to recovery for me was not without bumps and potholes. There were plenty of what I call "setbacks" along the way. I could have a week of good days, and then one day I might get panicky in a situation, and that panic monster would attack me. I might have a day or two of feeling terrible with all those weird physical symptoms hitting me. Dizziness, chest pains, head pains, stomach cramps, tremors and twitches were back. I may have had weeks without panic and then find myself at a red light going through my panic first aid kit, doing my breathing exercise and reciting my affirmations. My first instinct on these days was to rush right home to my safe zone and get into bed. These setback days often found me doing that very thing. Getting out of my safe zone and into the routine again was difficult after such an episode. I often felt hopeless after a day like that and wondered if I was ever going to get well. These setbacks made me wonder if panic was always going to be a part of my life. The first few setbacks were the worst. Some of the panic symptoms were so strong at times that I wondered if I was making progress at all. I couldn't let these setbacks stop me from getting well. Although it was very, very difficult, I made myself get back out there and persevere with my exposure goals. I found that if I let a setback keep me homebound for a few days, it was harder to get back into my routine, much like the bodybuilder taking a week off from weightlifting.

I had to change the way I thought about setbacks. Rather than looking at them as indicators of defeat, I treated them as milestones of progress. I planned on them, and as time went by, I started to look forward to them. I know that sounds strange. I looked forward to them because each time they came, they got weaker and weaker. They were becoming easier to overcome, and they were also coming less frequently. I began using setbacks as a way to monitor my progress. The first few came with very strong physical sensations, bordering on full blown panic attacks. These kept me down for days at a time. In a few months they came about once a week. Sometimes they came as panic. Other times they came as head pains or dizziness, but I did not let that develop into panic. Six months later, they came about once a month. A year later, they came maybe once every six weeks. By that time, they were almost nothing and didn't throw me off course at all. I remember having a setback day once and talking out loud as if I were talking to another person. I said, "Is that all you've got now?" These panic and anxiety symptoms that once had me crippled were now so weak that I barely gave them a second thought. I knew that the next setback was going to be so weak that I would laugh in its face. This was a game now. I was keeping score. I was winning. The ultimate victory was mine.

Once ruled by the grip of fear, I had now overcome this crippling condition. This experience was without a doubt the most devastating thing that had ever happened to me, or so I thought at the time. It was definitely the hardest thing I had ever been through. Panic had ruined me financially, socially, and mentally. If left alone, it would have ruined me in all areas of my life permanently. This whole experience had been a wake up call for me. Something was telling me that I could not go on living like

I was. This was my body's way of letting me know that. I got mad when I lost the ability to function normally, and that anger forced me to change. I decided that enough was enough. I made a plan and followed through with it. I had defeated this horrible thing without drugs, which was important to me. I got to the root of the problem and made changes in myself to ensure that this would never happen again. I was a different person now, confident that I could accomplish anything that I set my mind to.

I was also a more patient and compassionate person. For the first time in a long time, I felt like I was in control of my life and my destiny. I know without a doubt that I will never be a prisoner to fear again. I want everyone reading this book to have what I have, to beat panic and have the great life that is out there waiting. If I can do this, anyone can. I want my experience to be the glimmer of hope for you in your quest to get back to a normal life. You've read about how I did it. Now it's your turn.

# Your Plan for Recovery

I hope that by reading my story you can learn from my experience and apply my techniques to your own situation. Everyone is different. You may have slightly different fears, abilities, or symptoms. You may be able to drive a car but not go on a date. You may be able to speak to a group but not stand in a long line. You may never have full blown panic attacks but live in a constant state of heightened anxiety. Since everyone is different, I'm not going to try to lay out a specific step-by-step plan. I'm going to outline the general concepts and cover what I think are the basic strategies for getting well. You should take what you've read about my experiences and apply that information to your own circumstances. You may want to go back and read what I did on each of these items as you go through the outline. At the very minimum, write down your vision and goals. Now, let's get down to business and develop your plan for getting well.

**Develop a Vision.** What do you want out of this? What do you want to do? Visualize yourself doing it. Put it into words. Develop your personal vision of getting well and close your eyes and *be* that person. Get a clear vision of what you want and write it down. Read it out loud every day. Post it on your bathroom mirror, the refrigerator, and your nightstand. Become your vision.

**Be Patient.** Getting well is not going to happen overnight. This is going to take a while. Don't get discouraged if you do not see an immediate change. The key is to persevere. The progress will come.

**Make a Commitment.** Get mad. Have you had enough yet? Is living a life ruled by fear something that you are willing to accept? Decide that enough is enough and stick by your guns. Make a decision to change now.

**Find a Support Person**. Share your vision and your commitment with someone close to you. Keep this person informed of your progress. Let as many people around you know what you are going through and ask them to hang in there with you and support you as you beat this thing. You don't want to feel like you are doing this alone. Having a support person will help you get through the setbacks.

**Develop Your Panic First Aid Kit.** Use the tools in this kit to get through your panic attacks, or head them off at the pass before they turn into panic attacks. The first item in your kit should be your affirmations. These are words that give you comfort during those anxious times. Here are mine again. You're welcome to use these. Better yet, you should come up with your own that have special meaning to you.

> I am the same person right now as I am when I'm in my safe zone (I would visualize myself in my safe zone and feel the calmness that place brought to me).
>
> I am not having a heart attack.
>
> I am perfectly healthy. The doctors have told me so.
>
> I am not going to die from this.
>
> I am in control of my body and my thoughts.
>
> I am calm.
>
> I am at peace.

The next item in your kit should be the breathing technique. This helps you relax and focus when you start to feel panicky. Do this while reading your affirmations if you are trying to fight off a panic attack. This is also a great way to get to sleep at night if you are having trouble falling asleep.

> Slowly exhale all the air from your lungs through your mouth.

> Take a deep abdominal breath through the nose while counting to eight, filling the lungs. Be sure you are breathing from your lower abdomen. You can rest your hands just below your belly button and try to feel your gut pushing your hands away from your body as you breathe from your lower abdomen.

> Hold your breath while counting to eight again.

> Exhale through the mouth while counting to eight.

> Repeat two more times.

> Remember to inhale positive thoughts and exhale negative thoughts. Again, if you are fighting off a panic attack, use the affirmations as your positive thoughts.

**Don't Dwell on Fear.** Don't let fear or your obsession with this condition be the first thing you think of every day. The less time you give yourself to think about it, the less power it has over you. The next time you are tempted to think about fear, replace that thought with your vision.

Fear will be a thing of the past for you as long as you don't allow it any "air time" in your mind.

**Empty Your Stress Bucket.** Your stress bucket is your own personal capacity for stress. Keeping your bucket empty or at a low level makes you less likely to be panicky or anxious. Find out what's in your stress bucket and work on getting it emptied. Make a list of everything that's on your mind. Use this list as your "worry list." Designate a time to visit the list and worry. Otherwise, keep these things on the paper and not in your head. If they are in your head, they are in your bucket. Immediately cross off the items over which you have no control. Mentally flush these things and give them no more thought. Identify any of the top life stressors that you may have been through lately. These are part of the external stressors that are filling your bucket. Accept what you have control of and what you don't. Realize that they occupy space in your bucket. Visualize pouring them out of your bucket. Discover what you are doing to create the internal stressors in your bucket. These are things that you have control of. My bucket was full of internal stress because of what I considered personal flaws. I had to learn to say "no" to people, become assertive, and stop taking on more that I could do. I had to give up being a perfectionist. I also had to give up worrying about things that I had no control over. When you look at your worry list, take note of things that you bring on yourself. A lot of your stress could be self-inflicted. Make changes to stop adding internal stress to your bucket, even if it means saying "no" to other people or yourself. Delegate some of your responsibilities. You can't do it all! Remember that nothing is worth the price of your good health. This may mean that you'll have to make job or lifestyle changes.

**Set Your Exposure Goals.** If you're agoraphobic, you need to be able to do things and go places like everyone else. Set short-term and long-term goals that will expose you to things that you have come to avoid. Have a daily goal and keep it practical. Create an ultimate goal that will let you know without a doubt that you are well. Share these goals with your support person. Take it slow and stay just outside your comfort zone. Remember this is like bodybuilding. You will build up your ability to go places and do things until they become a natural part of your life again.

**Expect Setbacks.** You will have setbacks. Plan on them. Use them as a way to monitor your progress. They will come less often and will be less severe each time. This is a game, and setbacks are how you keep score. Each time you get back out of your safe zone after a setback is a victory.

These small victories will prevail, and you will come out as the winner!

**Watch What You Put In Your Mouth.** You absolutely must get completely off caffeine and alcohol. If it isn't already obvious why, caffeine causes nervousness. You want to eliminate as many things working against you as possible. The nervousness you get from using caffeine will make you more likely to feel panicky. This means avoiding most soft drinks, tea, coffee and chocolate. Alcohol is another thing to avoid because it has the same effect. There's no question that drinking a few beers or a glass of wine can take the edge off. The problem is that when the calming effects of alcohol wear off, you get the same type of rebound effect that you get from taking an anti-anxiety medication like Xanax. The more alcohol you drink, the more severe the rebound effect is. Lots of people have panic attacks the day after a drinking binge. If you're serious about getting well, lay off the things that will sabotage your efforts.

**Celebrate Your Victories.** Let your support person know about your goals and share your successes with that person. Each success is a step towards ultimate victory over panic and anxiety. You WILL win the game. You will accomplish your goals and they will be even more rewarding if you let your support person be part of the team.

# Claim Your New Life

As you're about to embark on this journey of changing your life for the better, you're probably just like I was – asking *Why me? Why do I have to go through this? This is not fair. I have been robbed of a normal life. I'm going to go through even more pain before it gets better. This is going to be a hard fight. Why can't I just roll back the clock and be normal again? After all, this whole thing seemed to come out of nowhere. I didn't even see it coming. How do I know that I'll get better? Maybe this is here to stay. Maybe this is what my life will be from now on.*

I'm here to tell you that if you want to get well bad enough, then you'll get well. This is a big wake up call. I could not go on living the way I was. This is why it happened. I wasn't just randomly selected to have panic and anxiety by some roll of the dice. Neither were you. This happened because I had reached my limit of handling stress. You have probably reached yours. This was my one big wake up call that has shaped the rest of my life. It will shape yours in ways you can't imagine. I am a different person now. I can see now that the whole experience was a huge blessing in disguise. I am now a goal-driven, confident, fearless, assertive person. At the same time, I'm also patient, compassionate, and calm. I handle stress in a much different way. I had once confused care with worry. Now I know how to care about things that are important without worrying about them. I also know how to have a fulfilling and rewarding life without feeling like I have to take on the world and please everyone along the way.

As you go through this journey of self-discovery, you will no doubt have changed your life for the better. It may not seem that way now, but once you come out as the victor in this game, you will look back and see how much better off you are for having been through this. I am here as the guy who has "been there, done that" to tell you that you will reap untold rewards from this experience. I believe you can do this. Get fed up. Make a decision. Change your life now. You have the power. You are in control. Now go out there and claim your new life!

For supporting information and companion workbook,
please visit www.panicfirstaid.com.

www.ingramcontent.com/pod-product-compliance
Lightning Source LLC
Chambersburg PA
CBHW020309290526
45784CB00003B/1438